In Remembrance of Me, Bearing Witness to Transgender Tragedy

In Remembrance of Me, Bearing Witness to Transgender Tragedy

An OtherWise Reflection Guide

Mx Chris Paige

OtherWise Engaged Publishing

Copyright © 2020 Chris Paige
All rights reserved.

No part of this book may be reproduced, distributed, or transmitted in any form by any means whatsoever without express written permission from the publisher, except in the case of brief quotations embodied in critical articles and reviews. Please refer all pertinent questions to the publisher.

First edition February 2020
Cover by Chris Paige
Cover image courtesy of Canva.com

ISBN: 978-1-951124-10-6 (Paperback)
ISBN: 978-1-951124-12-0 (Kindle)
eISBN: 978-1-951124-11-3
Audio ISBN: 978-1-951124-13-7

Published by OtherWise Engaged Publishing
http://otherwiseengaged4u.wordpress.com

Visit http://www.otherwisechristian.com

Dedicated to Minister Bobbie Jean Baker

All proceeds will be donated to
the Minister Bobbie Jean Baker Memorial Fund,
in support of the leadership of
Black transgender women

Table of Contents

Abbreviations
Introduction (1 Corinthians 11:24)

Chapter 1: Vigilance (2 Samuel 21:10)
Chapter 2: Observance (Lamentations 1:16)
Chapter 3: Reflection
Chapter 4: Bearing Witness (Matthew 26:38)
Chapter 5: Lamentation (Psalm 130:1–2)
Chapter 6: Resilience (James 4:10)
Chapter 7: Resistance (Ephesians 6:12)
Chapter 8: Repentance (Ezekiel 18:32)
Chapter 9: Hope (1 Thessalonians 4:13)

Afterword (Luke 10:29)

Appendix A: Four Reasons NOT to Host Transgender Day of Remembrance by Mx Chris Paige

Appendix B: Supporting Black Transgender Women

Appendix C: Liturgical Resources

We Gather by Louis Mitchell

Beatitudes, Re-imagined by Alexx Anderson and J Vu Mai

Embodied Remembrance: The Sacredness of Trans Day of Remembrance by RJ Robles

A Prayer with Black Transgender Women by Dee Dee Watters

Standing Against the Headwind of Hatred: A Prayer of Cisgender Confession and Commitment by Tammerie Day

Acknowledgements
OtherWise Reflection Guides
The OtherWise Christian series
About the Author: Mx Chris Paige
Praise for OtherWise Christian

Abbreviations

NIV   New International Version

ESV   English Standard Version

Introduction

> *[A]nd when he had given thanks, he broke [the bread] and said, "This is my body, which is for you; do this in remembrance of me."*
>
> **1 Corinthians 11:24 NIV**

As I compile these reflections, transgender communities have been holding vigils against anti-transgender violence on November 20 for twenty years now. That is long enough to have noticed patterns—not only about who is most frequently being killed, but also about how the rest of us are reacting to those deaths.

There are no quick fixes to the many factors involved in transgender tragedy, from intimate partner violence to economic insecurity. From gender to race to religion, there are many forces conspiring against us. There is so much work to be done. We feel so human and powerless in the face of it all. The temptations are many from going numb to turning away, from giving in to despair to sacrificing ourselves for the cause. Spiritual traditions have always been a rich resource for facing such overwhelming odds.

Rabbi Tarfon used to say: "It is not your duty to finish the work, but neither are you free to neglect it" (Pirkei Avot 2:16).

In this series of devotionals, you will be invited to reflect on themes that are related to Transgender Day of Remembrance (TDOR) in a variety of ways. Each chapter is relatively brief. Most open with a short scripture, include personal reflection questions, and close with a "You are loved" affirmation to help you ground yourself in strength.

My hope is that this volume will help you to organize yourself for the work that is yours to carry. My hope is that you will evaluate your own relationship, not only with TDOR as a "holiday," but also with transgender communities more generally.

How will you hold vigil with loved ones on or around TDOR?

How are transgender people and communities woven into your life year-round?

How will you allow yourself to be changed by the pain that you witness around you?

How do you make yourself available to those who are most at risk?

The proceeds from this book will go to support the leadership of Black transgender women, because the legacy of anti-transgender violence in the United States falls squarely (though not exclusively) on their shoulders. I want to be on record in every way possible saying that my sisters are so much more than victims or statistics. They are brilliant and they are wise. They are dynamic and they are powerful. They are fighting for survival, and we need more of their leadership and strength to help guide us through this next millennia.

Supporting the Minister Bobbie Jean Baker Memorial Fund is just one way that I work to support their leadership. More information about awards from the fund as well as mechanisms for making contributions can be found at http://www.transfaith.info.

In hope,

Mx Chris Paige
February 2020

Chapter 1

Vigilance

> *Then Rizpah the daughter of Aiah took sackcloth and spread it for herself on the rock, from the beginning of harvest until rain fell upon them from the heavens. And she did not allow the birds of the air to come upon them by day, or the beasts of the field by night.*
>
> **2 Samuel 21:10 ESV**

In 2 Samuel 21, Rizpah's two sons, Armoni and Mephibosheth, were killed by the Gideonites along with five more of Saul's sons. Essentially, they were killed in order to appease their deceased father's enemies. These seven potential heirs to the kingdom were killed, and then their bodies were left hanging in plain view on a hill.

While these deaths are gruesome in their way, it is the mourning and care of Rizpah for the deceased after their deaths that stands out in this story. Rizpah stands guard over the corpses for months, ensuring that neither the birds nor the animals would further desecrate the bodies. The time of this vigil is described as beginning with the harvest and continuing until the rains would come. Sources vary in their calculations of how long this would have been, ranging from four to seven months.

Regardless of the details of the political context, Rizpah lost two of her sons. In our modern world, we witness death in video games, documentaries, and all manner of movies. We dutifully review the death tolls from war and disease, from gun violence and hate crimes, and so much more. From social media to sound bites, it is almost impossible to take the time to process the news. We are almost inoculated against feeling anything. Yet, behind each of these statistics is someone's child—more than a number.

Rizpah is an example for all of us. She is assumed to be powerless in the face of this tragedy. She lived in a world that seemed ready to throw her children away over some political shenanigans. Yet, Rizpah defends her children's memory and honors their lives. In the face of their humiliating deaths, she does what she can to restore their dignity and to remember them—not because it will somehow bring her sons back but to embody the fundamental truth that their lives mattered.

Rizpah must have been filled with grief. Over those several months, surely those around her must have come along to tell her to "move on" or "get over it." She may have been consumed with anger and perhaps even contemplated revenge. Yet, she persevered in her attempt to salvage the dignity of her children. After her months of vigilance, King David gave all seven sons a proper burial. This in itself was not "success," but it was an acknowledgment.

On Transgender Day of Remembrance, we are faced with not just seven, but typically with at least 20 names in the United States alone—and each one is someone lost to anti-transgender violence. Behind each of these statistics is someone's child. Around the world, there are even more children who have died often brutal deaths by anti-transgender violence. Yet, these statistics do not begin to articulate further tragedies endured—from neglect to exploitation.

Often we hear that transgender women of color bear the brunt of such violence and, in the United States, the reported murders are overwhelmingly Black women. In a study of that violence, it was also revealed that the majority of these victims were under the age of 35. There are statistics around suicidality, homelessness, poverty, and more. In every case, young people are more at risk.

Each one of these young people is someone's child. We do not remember them because we are trying to bring them back—nor will our sorrow solve the many challenges facing transgender communities today. We remember them because we want to embody the fundamental truth that their lives matter—and we know that embracing this truth will change us. Indeed, these are our children, too. Like Rizpah, our ancestor in faith, let us remember each one, hold vigil, and demand care from the community.

How would you assess your commitment to support and defend transgender communities? Do you feel well equipped and connected? Do you need to seek out information or advisors to help build your confidence and insight? What are the next steps that you need to take to be more vigilant, like Rizpah?

You are loved. When you defend the children. In your grief and lamentation. When you refuse to forget. You are loved.

With gratitude for womanist theologians such as the Rev. Dr. Valerie Bridgeman, who recognized Rizpah's story as the story of so many grieving Black mothers, as well as for "Unerased: Counting Transgender Lives," a report from *Mic* that analyzed transgender murders from 2010 to 2016 (https://unerased.mic.com/).

YOUR NOTES

Chapter 2

Observance

> *For all these things I weep;*
> *tears flow down my cheeks.*
> *No one is here to comfort me;*
> *any who might encourage me are far away.*
> *My children have no future,*
> *for the enemy has conquered us.*
>
> **Lamentations 1:16**
> **New Living Translation**

Transgender Day of Remembrance (TDOR) is a very unusual "holiday." The tone and intention of the day can easily be misunderstood, especially by those who may be well-meaning, but new to transgender communities. Since 1999, TDOR has always been commemorated on November 20. However, observances may take place on the days or weekends before and/or after November 20 (depending on the day of the week on which November 20 occurs).

While other transgender-specific observances have been emerging in recent years, TDOR remains the single most significant observance on the calendar for transgender communities. TDOR is generally much more significant by far for transgender communities than other LGBT+ observances such as Pride Month or Coming Out Day or even Transgender Day of Visibility.

More like a memorial or funeral than any other kind of observance, the tone of TDOR observances reflects the impact that murder has on the tapestry of the transgender community as well as the very real lives of those who have been lost. Grief is the first response when loved ones are lost. TDOR creates a space to acknowledge that grief publicly, in a way that is similar to a funeral, a memorial service, or a wake. As such, you do not wait for an invitation to attend such an event. Instead, you watch for announcements of when and where you might go to pay your respects and offer support.

TDOR is also an act of resistance and a way to restore dignity. Too often, the murders of transgender people (especially of transgender women of color and those perceived as such) have included extreme violence, such as disfiguring and/or dismembering the victim. The rage apparent in such murders often embodies a hateful, terroristic impact that reverberates beyond the particular victim to humiliate and degrade the entire community. This is the definition of a "hate crime." TDOR services are places to acknowledge both the individual and collective impact of such extreme and humiliating violence—as well as to build resistance and restore dignity.

When transgender people are murdered, public outcry is often lacking. The cases all too often go unsolved. Even when the perpetrator is known, the criminal justice system may mark our lives as disposable by blaming the victim (for example, allowing the "trans-panic defense"). TDOR serves as a protest or vigil for justice around such unresolved grievances. It is a collective opportunity to respond to the neglect and uncaring attitudes of both the culture at large as well as authorities such as police and judicial systems more specifically. TDOR services offer a space for outrage. We demand accountability from authorities who have too often failed to protect our communities.

TDOR provides a way to become aware of who is most vulnerable in our communities. Over two decades of compiling names for TDOR, the annual lists of those who have been murdered overwhelmingly show that young transgender women of color bear the brunt of anti-transgender violence—even though there are a variety of risk factors that may impact each individual's ability to survive. TDOR is an opportunity to reflect on and repent of our roles in the systems that maintain these disparities. We must think again and again about how we might be more supportive to the communities that are most impacted.

Each year, we rise up out of isolation for support at TDOR services around the world. Those among us who have lost loved ones (or survived assault ourselves) have a particularly intimate relationship with trauma as a result of those experiences. Those of us who have not been directly impacted by these murders often still live in fear, suffer secondary trauma, and are in need of support as we process the all-too-familiar stories of lives "like us" that have been lost to violence. TDOR is an opportunity to come together and support one another as we face the challenges of ignorance, bigotry, and hatred aimed at people of transgender experience. It is important to recognize that the content of TDOR services may be triggering, so sensitive emotional support should be a part of what is offered to those present. A service that (re)traumatizes members of transgender communities is causing harm—even though it may be tempting to "shock" allies into action.

To be clear, TDOR is not a fundraiser or an outreach opportunity. As the most significant transgender observance of the year, it may be tempting to infuse all of one's hopes and dreams for connecting with the transgender community into this one day. Yet, TDOR is laced with a potent mix of grief and anger, fear and determination that ought not be conflated with other goals, no matter how noble or relevant. The vulnerability of TDOR should be acknowledged with sensitive support, not exploited for other ends. If your TDOR planning conversations are focused on how you will "find" transgender people to participate, then you should really reconsider hosting a TDOR service at all.

While often overlooked by allies, TDOR is an important opportunity to recommit to living with defiance, determination, and hope, despite the trauma we may have experienced and the fear that may haunt us. To say that TDOR may be inspiring is first to acknowledge the deep impact that violence has had on us and our communities. At TDOR, we reconnect with a warrior spirit that draws courage from the ancestors, so we might carry on for the children, both those who are among us and those who are yet to come.

This important day is an opportunity to connect with others who we might not otherwise get to know. For those of us who live in relative security and privilege, it is an opportunity to reach out to those who are most impacted by transphobia (and racism, sexism, ageism, and similar concerns), while nurturing authentic relationship, solidarity, and understanding. The connections made in and around TDOR services are starting points for continuing connections throughout the rest of the year. Research who else may be hosting TDOR services in your area. Attend those events in quiet support and see what new friends and colleagues you may encounter.

Have you ever attended a TDOR observance in your area? Who was in leadership? What was the mood and how did it feel for you to be there?

You are loved. When you are trying to understand. When you feel weary and wounded. When you are showing up outside your comfort zone. You are loved.

With gratitude for the Transfaith community, where I have learned so much about what does (and does not) matter. You can find my people at http://www.transfaith.info.

YOUR NOTES

Chapter 3

Reflection

*We must work
to put out the fire,
rather than merely watching
the smoke rise.*

J Mase III

In the United States, anti-transgender violence disproportionately impacts young Black transgender women. We need to take these trends seriously as we think about our own roles in Transgender Day of Remembrance (TDOR). Yet, these are not just statistical issues. They are also questions of relationship, segregation, and interdependence.

The way we experience TDOR is influenced by how we live our lives the other 364 days of the year. Who are we working with? Playing with? Collaborating with? Do we engage with any transgender friends, family, neighbors, or colleagues on a regular basis? Why or why not? Is TDOR the only day of the year that you are doing something intentional in support of transgender communities? Or does your TDOR observance flow naturally out of existing commitments and relationships?

In "Who Am I in Relationship to Transgender Day of Remembrance?" J Mase III puts a finer point on these questions. Many of us engage with certain kinds of people of transgender experience, but not others—and those differences matter.

> Many trans feminine people are impacted daily by this violence differently than even their trans masculine counterparts as they move in a world that devalues womanhood. People of color are impacted by this violence differently than their non-POC counterparts as they move in a

> world that privileges whiteness. Differently-abled folks experience this violence uniquely as they move in a world that denies the personal agency of many based on perceived or actual physical and/or mental ability. (J Mase III)

In addition, economic, employment, and housing privileges are key factors that mitigate many other risk factors.

TDOR observances often reveal our priorities as well as the on-going disconnects between different aspects of transgender communities. If you are not already working closely with transgender women of color, then TDOR may be an important opportunity to show up some place that is new to you.

> Are there trans organizations in your area that will be hosting a Transgender Day of Remembrance event? If so, is it possible that you and/or your organization could support their efforts? If there are no Transgender Day of Remembrance services in your area, do you understand why? (J Mase III)

Do your activities on and around TDOR demonstrate your distance from or your connections with transgender communities? Which transgender communities are you most familiar with? Which transgender communities do you need to learn more about?

Those of us who are less at risk tend to be more accustomed to taking charge, leading the way, and being the center of attention. Yet, TDOR is not about us. TDOR should be a time when we are intentionally rallying around those who are most at risk. It can take real work and reflection to shift our energies toward supporting others, if that is not already a part of our daily life, but doing so will open up the possibility of more authentic relationships.

How will your energies around TDOR be connected to year-round transgender organizing in your area? How will your presence build more inclusive relationships among the living? How can you nourish, support, and celebrate a more dynamic resistance among transgender women of color, specifically?

You are loved. When you are stretching. When you are reaching out. When you are making space to support the work of others. You are loved.

With gratitude for J Mase III's "Is your Transgender Day of Remembrance a 'one-night stand' or a larger commitment?" and "Who am I in Relationship to Transgender Day of Remembrance? Critical Questions for Organizers." You can find both articles at http://www.transfaith.info.

YOUR NOTES

Chapter 4

Bearing Witness

> *Then [Jesus] said to them,*
> *"My soul is overwhelmed with sorrow to the point of death.*
> *Stay here and keep watch with me."*
>
> **Matthew 26:38 NIV**

It is perhaps natural for religious folk to want to pray for and with transgender people, especially around tragedies like those we remember on Transgender Day of Remembrance. However, it is important to remember that the rhetoric of prayer has been complicated by years of Christian trans-antagonism. In fact, "prayer" has often been used as a weapon against transgender people.

Many trans folk have left their religious traditions of origin because of experiences of spiritual abuse. From reparative therapy to exorcism, from ex-communication to words such as "pervert" or "abomination," many transgender people have been physically, emotionally, and spiritually punished for telling the truth about our lived experience. This is frequently done under the guise of religious authorities such as "God," "faith," or "the Bible." Sometimes, our abusers specifically say that they are "praying for us" while they are actively causing us harm.

These kinds of lived experiences contribute to feelings of isolation and the feeling of being a burden—which are two major risk factors for a trans person attempting to end their own life. According to the 2015 U.S. Transgender Survey, well over 40% of trans people have attempted suicide at least once, as compared to the roughly 5% of the general population. The research shows that this extremely high rate is primarily due to stress caused by other people, not because of any problem inherent to being transgender.

From Confucius to the Qur'an, most religious traditions teach the Golden Rule in some form, which means putting yourself into the other's shoes before taking action. "Praying for" trans people can be well-meaning, but it may also send a dangerous message. Prayer can be experienced as another form of assault and spiritual trauma. Religious people concerned with transgender justice need to understand this context before they rush into prayer "for" transgender communities.

Of course, I am not asking religious folk to cease praying if that is your personal practice. I am just asking you to be sensitive in terms of how you make those prayers visible. In fact, people of faith typically have tremendous experience and expertise when it comes to supporting others in times of tragedy. Yet, it is not uncommon to hear from helpline callers or even transgender friends on social media, "Nobody cares if we live or die." Political shenanigans and social media arguments about transgender folk often enhance this kind of doubt and despair.

Please understand that transgender communities are often carrying a great deal of pain. Like Jesus in the garden before his death, we are facing brutal violence under an occupying empire, and there is no quick fix. Jesus' request as he faced death points to the discipline of offering our presence to one another. He asked for loved ones to gather around him to bear witness and be in community through his struggles.

Stay awake with us. Keep watch. Be present.

Like Jesus, we ask those close to us to pray *with* us, when asked. Not *for* us. Not *about* us. But *with* us.

Showing up in authentic relationship is a life-saving practice, even when you do not have answers or a quick fix. Of course, we also need allies who will storm the barricades and make a scene. We need help challenging the Empire. That is important and essential political and cultural work. Still, it can be tempting to rush too quickly toward "action," while losing sight of the very people that you say you care about.

I worked with colleagues from the Trans Lifeline on "An Open Letter to Our Allies about What We Really Need from You." They shared:

> Operators with the Trans Lifeline hear the stories and the pain. We help these conflicted callers by creating a safe space to voice their pain, their

> fears, their injuries. Sometimes we offer remedies, but the biggest thing is presence; creating a space for callers to vocalize that which they are prevented from saying in other places.
>
> A number of trans clergy and other trans spiritual leaders who work with Trans Lifeline are doing this as sacred work. We never "preach" and don't engage spiritual concerns unless specifically asked by our callers. To do so would be to commit the very assault we lament. ("Open Letter to Our Allies," March 23, 2017)

Still, it makes a tangible difference when loved ones take the time to lament with us, to sit with us, to visit with us, to join with us. This is bearing witness in the best sense of the phrase. It can be hard, messy, emotional work, but offering the gift of your presence as we struggle through the challenges that we face can make a real difference.

We are afraid. We are grieving murdered friends and friends bullied to suicide. Many of us grapple with despair every day. We are recovering from physical, emotional, and spiritual violence—often even from service providers who have pledged to care for us. Please do not make us continue to face these dark nights alone.

Many of us have lost our families of origin. While this loss may make the holidays more tedious, its impact during other times of tragedy and loss is even more intense. An invitation to your family gathering may be worth offering where appropriate, but you should also understand that such gatherings may be anxiety-producing or exhausting if your family is not already a familiar and trans-competent resource. Making time to show up when you know your friend is struggling with grief, anxiety, or loss is much more important.

Unemployment, poverty, and homelessness are serious concerns for our community, in part because we have not been able to depend on birth families as a reliable safety net or even as an affirming resource. The world can be a scary place to navigate on your own. For many of us, having a witness to go with us makes visiting the doctor a possibility, instead of an anxiety-ridden ordeal. Even using the bathroom can be dicey for many of us.

You do not have to be a service provider, and you do not have to fix "all of the things" in order to make a difference in someone's life. You just have to have the courage to be a friend. Sharing a meal, bringing a casserole, or watching a movie together can be a life-saving ministry during times when despair and isolation may be lurking. The truth is that you probably already have a lot of experience at being a supportive friend or family member!

Do not be afraid to ask the most important question of all, "How can I best support you?" Sometimes this question is so surprising that it may take time for us to find an answer. So be patient. As long as you are being authentic and not anxiously trying to get your transgender "merit badge," you can keep asking and offering. Make yourself available. Be creative. Be a friend.

Who might you reach out to with a word of encouragement or support? How can you make yourself more available today?

You are loved. When you make yourself available. When your life is woven together with those in need. You are loved.

With gratitude for the work of Dr. Donovan Ackley III, Z Shane Zaldivar, and colleagues who work daily at Trans Lifeline and other transgender-competent service providers. "An Open Letter to Our Allies about What We Really Need from You" can be found at http://www.transfaith.info.

YOUR NOTES

Chapter 5

Lamentation

> *From the depths of my despair*
> *I call to you, LORD.*
> *Hear my cry, O Lord;*
> *listen to my call for help!*
>
> **Psalm 130:1–2**
> **Good News Translation**

We live in a society where many of us have not been taught how to grieve or lament. We are a quick-fix culture that so often emphasizes retail therapy and medical interventions. Obscene amounts of money are spent on advertising campaigns to inform us that there is a solution to our every problem (if we just purchase the appropriate product).

I was raised in a nice Protestant Christian home where hard work was valued. While there are many kinds of Christian culture, I learned that "God helps those who help themselves." I am as prone as anyone else to encourage a friend or colleague to "hang in there" and "keep on keeping on." Rarely do we encourage one another to stop entirely.

In "Resilience through the Practice of Lament," Dr. Koach Frazier reminds us that grief work is important. He says, "How can the healing process begin, if we have never stopped to acknowledge that healing is actually necessary?" Spiritual and emotional processes like grief and lamentation often short-circuit because "bereavement leave" is over, and we are told, directly or indirectly, that it is time to "move on."

As a Black transgender Jew who is from Ferguson, Missouri, Frazier is all too familiar with communities that have experienced relentless tragedy. He reminds us how important it is to listen to our own sorrow and pain. He says, "When we mourn, we stop time. We don't go to work. We do not go to school. ... We cannot have business as usual when tragedy strikes."

Frazier does not shame us for being inexperienced at grieving. He helpfully suggests a four-step formula for lament.

The first step is the address—calling out to God, the Universe, the Source of All Life, or whatever you might call your helping powers. This helps us to shift into reaching out beyond ourselves.

The second step is to express our distress—naming that which is causing us pain. For instance, "Why are my siblings dying?" or "How long, God, how long?" It is essential that we give voice to that which brings us grief and sorrow, rather than hiding our pain.

In the third step, we remember. We remember that we are still here, surviving, even as we struggle. This is an important step that can help us not to lose ourselves in despair. We have seen tragedy before and we have made it through—both individually and collectively.

The fourth step is a plea—naming what it is that we need in order to begin healing. Asking for what we need is itself a spiritual discipline and one that is not consistently encouraged in mainstream culture. In his live presentation, Frazier breaks into a chorus of "Be with me" which speaks to our need for community and accompaniment. Being specific helps us just as much as anyone who might be listening.

Of course, this formula for lament is not a quick fix. We still have to take time to do the grief work, to experience our feelings, to connect with our bodies, and to make space to allow the pain to move through us. Yet, this formula is one tool we can use to support ourselves when we are overwhelmed. It is a way we can connect with both God and our ancestors in faith, whether we lament in private or in community.

Have you been taught to grieve through family, religious, or cultural traditions? How do you make space to process change, grief, and death when these themes touch your life?

You are loved. When you take time to slow down. When you name your pain and express your sorrow. When you allow yourself to be human. You are loved.

With gratitude for Dr. Koach Baruch Frazier who is currently a student at the Reconstructionist Rabbinical College, near Philadelphia, PA. His speech "Resilience through the Practice of Lament" was presented at Speak Torah to Power in May 2019 and is available for viewing on YouTube (https://www.youtube.com/watch?v=PcaTaXK_kyI).

YOUR NOTES

Chapter 6

Resilience

*Humble yourselves before the Lord,
and he will lift you up.*

James 4:10 NIV

In the last year, I have aged a lot. It turns out that I became middle-aged when I was not looking. In my younger years, I learned to push my way through athletic endeavors and academic challenges. I learned that friends and allies "show up" for others no matter what. In fact, these are lessons that helped me to be successful both personally and professionally in many ways.

Resilience is often framed in this way, as being about whether we can or cannot "keep going" no matter what. However, in this new season of my life, I am finally learning to slow down. I am a parent, an author, an employee, and a church volunteer. I have had a couple of situations where I pushed hard to "show up" and ended up losing my temper. Of course, I could point my finger at what the other people involved might have done differently to change the situation (and I might not be wrong). However, the bottom line is that I "showed up" on a day when I was not well equipped to be resilient in community.

Realizing this has been a real challenge to my values! Christianity talks a lot about sacrifice. I have been indoctrinated to push, push, push myself "for the greater good." Yet, I am starting to learn more about saying "No," since my body has been slowing down at the same time that my personal commitments have become more complicated.

Often, saying "No" and setting boundaries is framed around self-care. Western culture is steeped in the values of individualism. However, "taking care of myself" only helps me to make different choices in the most extreme situations (for example, utter exhaustion).

In my more day-to-day discernment, it has helped me more to remember that I am not God.

Now, don't worry. I do not consciously struggle with the idea that I might *be* God. However, when I push, push, push myself well beyond my limits, it is partly because I am trying to be more than myself—more than human. In other words, I am trying to be some kind of superhero, who is not acknowledging my human limitations. There is some (unintentional) arrogance mixed in with the assumption that I should be able to accomplish every thing, all of the time.

In order to support myself in making different choices, it helps me to remember that I am not God and that I can trust both my community and my Creator to get along without me, at least some of the time. I have come to realize that it is a little bit self-centered to imagine that I am so important that no one can live without me, even if only while I take a day off to rest or recover.

I am still living into this new revelation, but it speaks to me about resilience in the midst of the many tragedies facing transgender communities, specifically, and the world at large, more generally. It can be useful, fruitful, productive, and even responsible to take time away from our day-to-day activities, to breath, to heal, to slow down, and to reconnect. In fact, our times of busy-ness and struggle may be the most important times for us to check our limitations.

Bearing witness in the midst of tragedy necessarily means learning to accept and live into loss. It is still not easy for me to admit my own limits, but it is also a blessing to realize that I get to be human. I can weep and rage and fall asleep early and not always "show up" for everything. I get to be human because I do not have to be God. God has that one covered. This, too, is resilience.

Are there ways that you need to let go of unreasonable expectations or control? How might you do more to honor your own limitations? How could you do less in a way that might actually help the cause?

You are loved. When you are struggling to keep going. When you realize that you need to take some time away to replenish. When you are resting. You are loved.

With gratitude for Living Water United Church of Christ (Philadelphia, PA) where God is God and I have been learning how to be more human.

YOUR NOTES

Chapter 7

Resistance

> *For our struggle is not against flesh and blood,*
> *but against the rulers, against the authorities,*
> *against the powers of this dark world*
> *and against the spiritual forces of evil*
> *in the heavenly realms.*
>
> **Ephesians 6:12 NIV**

Transgender Day of Remembrance (TDOR) is not a "celebration" kind of holiday but, rather, a time set aside for lamentation and resistance. In transgender communities, when we remember our beloved dead, our siblings, our loved ones, our children, who have been lost to anti-transgender violence, we are doing more than compiling statistics. We are reclaiming our history and re-membering our community in the face of ongoing violence and humiliation, particularly against young transgender women of color.

The National Day of Mourning occurs shortly after TDOR each year and has many parallels. Created as an alternative to the (U.S.) Thanksgiving "holiday," the National Day of Mourning is a

> reminder of the genocide of millions of Native people, the theft of Native lands, and the relentless assault on Native culture. Participants in National Day of Mourning honor Native ancestors and the struggles of Native peoples to survive today. It is a day of remembrance and spiritual connection as well as a protest of the racism and oppression which Native Americans continue to experience. (United American Indians of New England website at http://uaine.org)

As a transgender person of European descent and Christian upbringing, it is important to my own growth and healing for me to lean into the connections between these two observances.

When European settler-colonists first came to what we now call North America, they brought a potent triple threat of white supremacy, Christian supremacy, and gender-based oppression. Our colonial legacy carefully weaves these three powerful forces together, through both violence and indoctrination. In other words, colonization is not just something that "happened" to Native peoples several hundred years ago. It is a dynamic force that continues today, shaping how we think about religion, race, and gender in every aspect of our world.

To heal from this inheritance, we must do more than simply express regret and move on. We need to unpack and examine the ways that this legacy continues to shape us and our relationships even today. It is a colonial legacy that certain kinds of violence are applauded as "security" and others condemned as "savagery." Some victims are perceived as "innocent" and others as "suspicious." This same legacy calls "deviant," "sinful," or "sick" any of us who exist or veer outside the bounds of Western gender norms that demand we conform to two and only two mutually exclusive gender narratives.

While white feminist trajectories (including gay, lesbian, and transgender aspects) have long attempted to separate gender issues from race issues, transgender women of color live at the brutal intersection of all three of these streams of violence (that is, racial, religious, and gendered violence). The lists of names and descriptions of violent deaths that are memorialized on TDOR are what colonization "looks like" in public—that is, the triple threat deployed in full force on Black and Brown OtherWise-gendered bodies, topped off with bountiful waves of self-righteous victim-blaming.

TDOR itself is an example of how colonization is alive and well in our world today. The stories of transgender women of color are too often colonized by white transgender communities, as well as observed by cisgender people as a kind of trauma porn. The energy released from acknowledgements of anti-transgender violence is too often deployed in support of other hardly related aims. Well-meaning, liberal-minded Christian communities, too, take part in this appropriation as we host TDOR services without fully grappling with the ways this multifaceted legacy shapes our relationships with the communities that we say we want to serve.

It is not enough for us to grieve and lament—though that is surely part of what we must do in response to these centuries of violence, assault after assault on the humanity of our siblings. It is not enough to talk about the criminal (in)justice system and how it does or does not identify or punish perpetrators of violence. We can talk about cultural change, restorative practices, reparations, and intersectionality—and we must—but it will never be enough until we also begin to claim and sort through this legacy of colonization.

I am a non-binary, transgender person of European descent and Christian upbringing. I am and will always be in recovery from white supremacy, Christian supremacy, and oppressive Western ideas about gender. I claim my identity, not because I am proud of this history of exploitation and violence. Rather, I claim this history as my own because this is the legacy that I have inherited, because this is the healing that our ancestors still long for, because this is the true story shaping the ways we can (and cannot) build deeper solidarity with one another.

For those of us who share this legacy, we must remember that the land on which we sit, stand, and sleep was stolen and exploited for us. These kinds of violations continue to be perpetrated, now by corporations and government agencies rather than by *conquistadors*.

We must remember that bodies, too, were stolen and exploited for us. These kinds of violations also continue to be perpetrated—not by the exact same kind of plantation politics, but by systems of mass incarceration, corporate-driven economies, and even non-profit industrial complexes that still find a plethora of ways to extract resources and exploit labor.

It is not just two spirit people who were torn asunder—both suppressed from their communities of origin and torn limb from limb. This legacy of colonial systems targeting OtherWise-gendered people of color continues today as two spirit, transgender, intersex, queer, and non-binary people of color continue to bear the brunt of violence and exploitation in so many ways.

Reflections like this are difficult in that there is so much that needs to be said and no simple action step to propose that will quickly decolonize our society from this triple threat ("Just vote NO on colonization and all will be well!"). It is too much of a Gordian knot, intertwined and tangled with our history, institutions, cultural expressions, and worldviews. The more we pull on one thread, the more another may be tightened. We will need to work together on this project from many angles before we have any hope of breaking free.

We need one another now, more than ever.

Yet, before we can fully make that collective work our own, we must admit that we are all bound by this legacy. We must fully claim who we are as descendants of this legacy of violence and indoctrination. It is not "fair" and I do not have to "like it." Of course, it is uncomfortable (as well it should be), but white supremacy, Christian supremacy, and the oppression of OtherWise-gendered people are my inheritance nonetheless. Even a lifetime of immersion in nice, white, liberal culture does nothing to change this fact.

How do you embrace difficult truths in your life? How do you hold fast even when things are dangerous, uncomfortable, or overwhelming?

You are loved. When you refuse to turn away from the truth. When you seek to restore and repair. You are loved.

With gratitude to many two spirit siblings who have bravely worked in so many ways to reclaim their places in traditional communities, as well as for the work of Dr. Cornel West who said, "Never forget that justice is what love looks like in public."

YOUR NOTES

Chapter 8

Repentance

> *For I take no pleasure*
> *in the death of anyone,*
> *declares the Sovereign LORD.*
> *Repent and live!*
>
> **Ezekiel 18:32 NIV**

Facing transgender tragedy can bring up all manner of difficult feelings. If we do not deal with our own feelings about those tragedies, they are likely to come out in other ways. This dynamic has many, often unintentional, consequences. Too often, those unresolved emotions get directed at the folk who are struggling the most.

Feelings of guilt and shame are often a first response to learning about systems of oppression. Such feelings are not the answer, but they may be a stepping stone. Our ancestor, Black lesbian poet warrior, Audre Lorde, wrote more than 35 years ago:

> Guilt is not a response to anger; it is a response to one's own actions or lack of action. If it leads to change then it can be useful, since it is then no longer guilt but the beginning of knowledge. Yet all too often, guilt is just another name for impotence, for defensiveness destructive of communication; it becomes a device to protect ignorance and the continuation of things the way they are, the ultimate protection for changelessness. (Audre Lorde, "The Uses of Anger," 1981; printed in Sister Outsider, 1984)

In the relentless churning of a broken world, it can be easy to get stuck. How do we get through it, and where do we go?

Repentance is said to be about turning around or changing course. We are living in the midst of systems that cause harm, often in ways that are beyond our control as individuals. Repentance is neither about "feeling bad" nor about being "forgiven." Repentance is about allowing ourselves to be changed by our proximity to the harm, instead of continuing on about our normal business insulated from those realities.

I believe the first step of repentance is getting comfortable with being uncomfortable. There is a difference between being harmed and being uncomfortable. Grief and anger are uncomfortable. Guilt and shame are uncomfortable. Unresolved problems beyond our control are uncomfortable because they leave us feeling powerless and inadequate.

Yet, these are all just feelings. Working in the midst of these kinds of uncomfortable feelings is essential to being a productive part of resistance movements. We have to learn to weather such emotional challenges, if we want to be relevant to folk who are struggling (even if the one struggling is you). The trick is working with those feelings, not just wallowing in them. We can start by fully feeling the feelings and letting them move through our bodies.

What if we commit to lamenting the many ways the world around us harms our people? What if we let our discomfort drive us toward changing the way we think and feel about the world in which we live? How will your life be different because of the names that are read on Transgender Day of Remembrance? How will your life be different because you know how prevalent thoughts of suicide are in transgender communities?

Marginalized communities grapple with these kinds of challenges every day, resolute in fighting death and despair, clinging to our humanity against all odds. Are you ready to join us?

Repentance means that we are not just watching the head count and continuing about our business as usual. We are allowing the pain to touch us, change us, and shape us—both our sense of self and our commitments. It allows us to be softer and more vulnerable with one another as we are filled with compassion. It also empowers us to be stronger and more determined as our commitment to one another grows deeper.

Repentance means that we are willing to offer more than just an emotional transaction in order to make ourselves more comfortable. Wading into the discomfort means that we are choosing not to stand idly by as an observer or consumer of the tragedies before us. Instead, we bring ourselves all the way into relationship. In repentance, we are investing in change, starting with our own lives.

This repentance is not "pat me on the back" superhero change. Nor is it Nobel Peace Prize global impact change. No cookies will be distributed for learning how to be human in the face of tragedy. However, keeping a firm hold on our humanity in the face of a world full of pain and violence *is* that critical first step in being relevant. Once we allow ourselves to be changed, we become ready to do the unique work that is ours to do—to move from comfort and avoidance through discomfort and grief, to join more authentically in solidarity with our kindred.

How have you already been changed by bearing witness to transgender tragedy? Are there ways you already know you want to shift further? How will you open yourself to further change, whether internally or externally?

You are loved. When you are uncomfortable. When you are feeling the feelings. When you are allowing yourself to be changed by this broken world. You are loved.

With gratitude for Dr. Audre Lorde's many calls to feeling deeply: "For having experienced the fullness of this depth of feeling and recognizing its power, in honor and self-respect we can require no less of ourselves" ("Uses of the Erotic: The Erotic as Power" by Dr. Audre Lorde, 1978; printed in *Sister Outsider*, 1984).

YOUR NOTES

Chapter 9

Hope

> *[Siblings], we do not want you to be uninformed*
> *about those who sleep in death,*
> *so that you do not grieve*
> *like the rest of [hu]mankind,*
> *who have no hope.*
>
> **1 Thessalonians 4:13 NIV**

  Twenty years of being connected to transgender communities has changed me. It has not given me all of the answers, but it has definitely changed my questions. There is no place where this shift in me is more poignant than in how it has changed my relationship with death.

  Minister Bobbie Jean Baker is a transgender sister. I met her through the TransSaints ministry of the Fellowship of Affirming Ministries, and we stayed connected through national conferences and other gatherings. You can hear her voice in the documentary movie *The Believers* or in music from the historic Transcendence Gospel Choir. Bobbie Jean passed unexpectedly early on New Year's Day 2014. She did not die from suicide or from anti-transgender violence. She did not die from neglect or poverty or inadequate health care or any of the issues that so frequently frame transgender tragedy. It was a car accident caused by a drunk driver.

  It still shook me. I woke to the news. I wept in my bed. I was not in especially close contact with Bobbie Jean, though I recorded our last conversation because I was going to write about a project she was working on. We lived on opposite ends of the continent. We were both busy.

  Bobbie Jean could have been anyone. She could have been any New Year's Eve traffic accident tragedy, but she was not just anyone.

She was *my* friend. She was someone *I* worked with. She was someone whose voice was familiar to *me*. She was someone who helped make me *more* real, *more* authentic, *more* human. It still makes my chest hurt to think of her as I write this. She is not just anyone. She is not just a rapidly fading memory. She is a part of me

I do not know if it was the loss of Bobbie Jean. Or Charlene. Or Lois. Or some other friend or colleague. I do not know if it was my tending to a conversation about someone else's suicidal intentions—or someone else tending to a conversation about my own despair. But at some point, I realized that it matters for us to remember one another. I realized in deeper ways that we re-member one another—that we put one another back together when things fall apart. Sometimes in life. Sometimes in death. This remembering matters.

Some time along the way, Jesus' words to his friends took on new life for me. "Do this in remembrance of me" (1 Corinthians 11:24b). Broken bodies. Shared meals. Lingering conversations. Friends remembering. Like Jesus, our OtherWise-gendered ancestors (some say transcestors) have been through it, too. Betrayal. Loss. Violence. Neglect. Rejection. Shame. Trying to figure how to keep going when there seems to be nothing left to hope for.

Despite what you may have been told, we do not journey through this life on our own. Some companions may hurt us. Some companions may help us. Probably most do at least a little bit of both. Yet, even when living humans may seem to have forsaken us, the ancestors are always standing by, bearing witness to our trials and tribulations and lighting our way. We are not the first. We will not be the last. Herein lies my hope.

Communities that suffer great tragedy often feel a stronger connection to our ancestors. Transgender communities are no different, except that we have less of a shared, inter-generational culture upon which to draw for our re-membering. We are never alone. Even if our connection to blood relatives may be compromised, we live under the watchful eye of those who came before us. The saints are yet with us as a cloud of witnesses (Hebrews 12:1).

Protestant Christianity has taught many of us to worry way too much about beliefs. You may or may not believe in "God." You may or may not believe in "heaven" or "hell." You may or may not believe in the "ancestors" as people who we can relate to across time. But, I am not trying to convince you of any of those things. I simply offer my testimony about the power of community—Christian community, transgender community, communities of friends and relations, whether by blood or by love. Such communities are an ancestral tradition. They are a legacy passed on from one generation to another.

I believe that honoring our dead can change the way we live. The meaning in our lives is not actually created by ideologies or institutions but, rather, by and for and with the people and communities than surround us—including those who have gone on before us. We are woven into one another like threads in a rope. We make one another stronger when we hold each other close.

I do not remember Jesus because Jesus *needs* me to remember. I do not remember our transgender ancestors because they *need* me to remember them. I remember because it changes me. It moves me. I remember them because they are a part of me. May their memory be a blessing.

No, really. May we open ourselves up so that we might be blessed by their memory. May we break bread with them. May we say their names. May we sing their songs. May we honor their struggles as stories which are connected to our own. May we never forget.

Do this in remembrance of me. Not because of some charitable impulse. Not because of some sad, sappy story. Not because of some manipulative sense of obligation. But because we *need* one another.

In my last reflection about bearing witness to transgender tragedy, you might expect a rousing call to action. But, no. Once you take the time to lament, to feel, to be changed by the violence—once you commit to a practice of remembering and bearing witness and re-membering—you will not be able to avoid taking action. I do not need to tell you what those actions will be. It will depend on who you are, where you make community, and what your capabilities are. It will depend on the unique opportunities that present themselves to you.

If you feel deeply connected to those who have suffered, I am confident that you will find your way. Grieve, but do not grieve like those who have no hope. Do not be uninformed about those who sleep in death. Those who sleep are still our community. Weave them into your living. Do this in remembrance of them. Do this in remembrance of Jesus. Someday, I will be gone. Do this in remembrance of me, too. Weave each one of us into your living. This, too, is hope.

How will you remember?

You are loved. When you remember. When you honor those who have gone before you. When you claim your ancestors. You are loved.

With gratitude for the life of my friend, Minister Bobbie Jean Baker; for the wisdom of my teacher, Dr. Daniel Foor; and for all the saints who have helped me move beyond worrying about "what I believe" into the strength of community with our ancestors.

YOUR NOTES

Afterword

> *But he wanted to justify himself,*
> *so he asked Jesus,*
> *"And who is my neighbor?"*
>
> **Luke 10:29 (NIV)**

There is good reason to talk about the tragedies that haunt young Black transgender women. It is important to talk about those who are most impacted by particular kinds of violence. These trends help us to identify patterns in behaviors, communities in need of resources, and interventions that may be most helpful. We can only reflect on our relationship with such violence if we take such a step back from individual circumstances to look at trends.

However, each one of us is unique. When we bear witness to transgender tragedy, we engage with actual people, not statistics—and there is plenty of tragedy to go around. Despair lurks around the corner from every microaggression, broken heart, or question about who may or may not be trustworthy. Rejection breeds not only loneliness but often also lack of housing, lack of resources, and lack of options. When we are on our own and pressed beyond our limits, risk-taking that might otherwise seem unthinkable begins to look like opportunity. Circumstances conspire.

Black. Man. Sex worker. White. Woman. HIV+. Latinx. Non-Binary. Disabled. Asian. Genderqueer. Abuse survivor. Native American. Gender Non-Conforming. Orphan. Middle Eastern. Intersex. Trauma survivor. Clergy. Immigrant. Veteran. Unhoused. Unemployed. Undocumented. Uninsured. Uneducated.

We live in a world that is defined by "identity" in so many ways. While words and categories may help us to make sense out of a complex world, they can also prevent us from really hearing one another's testimony. Tragedy tends to happen at the intersections, in the gaps, and between our best intentions. We need to listen, stay awake, pay attention, and remember that tragedy takes many forms.

Not all will register or be easily identified in a review of surface disclosures.

Each of us has the opportunity to bear witness for, to intervene on behalf of, and to impart hope to one another. The call is to love, not to rescue—but to love is to be in relationship. To be in relationship is to experience the rhythms, textures, and character of one another's lives. We must listen for the way that not just full-blown tragedy but each and every loss may shape our future options and choices.

In Luke 10, when the lawyer asked Jesus about his neighbor, Jesus responded by pointing to the need for empathy. We are good neighbors when we are in relationship, when we feel something, when we experience intimacy with those who are suffering, when we are filled with mercy and compassion. This is what Jesus asks of us. May we go and do likewise.

You are loved. When you connect. When you listen. When you care. You are loved.

Appendix A

Four Reasons Not to Host Transgender Day of Remembrance
by Chris Paige

1. Transgender Day of Remembrance (TDOR) should be observed first and foremost for and with living transgender people.

If you are not in active relationships with transgender people throughout the year, then TDOR is, literally, a sad place to begin your outreach and advocacy. Remember, TDOR is a day about trauma. It is about acknowledging violent, often gruesome, deaths of transgender people. Your first steps of outreach should be about connecting with and investing in the living, not focusing on our dead.

2. TDOR is not a competitive sport.

Many—if not most—cities have community TDOR services organized and led by local transgender leaders. By creating another separate TDOR service, you may be drawing support away from existing transgender leadership.

Remember, TDOR services are more like funerals than almost any other kind of "holiday." You do not need to wait for an invitation to attend a community-led TDOR service. It is often most appropriate for you to go to pay your respects and offer the gift of your presence to the already gathered community than it is to plan your own separate service.

3. Staging a TDOR service without involving transgender people

is "trauma tourism."

If your TDOR service does little to nothing to change the material conditions of the transgender communities you claim to support, then it may actually serve as a kind of emotional exploitation—even if you totally mean well.

Like the emotional release that comes from watching a horror film, being a spectator to an annual review of the deaths of transgender people may serve as a kind of emotional escapism that lets you feel like you are connected without having to get too close. It can become a distraction that prevents you from channeling that energy and concern into doing something more relevant for (or *with*) the transgender communities in your area.

4. TDOR is not supposed to be comfortable.

While it is a positive sign of increased awareness that TDOR has become a recognized "holiday" in the canon of liberal causes, we are now at risk of allowing TDOR to become another opportunity for self-segregation—for us to retreat again into insular spaces with familiar people.

Research into murders of transgender people shows that anti-transgender violence overwhelmingly impacts young Black transgender women. Most churches are not anywhere near the neighborhoods where young Black transgender women congregate. TDOR is a great opportunity to get out of your comfort zone to connect with those people, communities, and organizations that are better connected—and this advice goes for white transgender people, too!

Of course, there are also lots of good reasons to host a TDOR service, especially if it will be meaningful to transgender people in your congregation, if your local community does not have anyone hosting a TDOR service, and if transgender people in your community are asking you to host a service. But, please do not let TDOR be just another day to make yourself comfortable by going through the motions.

What might you do instead of a hosting a TDOR service?

Here are a few ideas:

Rally members of your congregation to go together to a TDOR service led by transgender people in the community. Take the first steps toward building new relationships in your community.

Take an offering to support a cause that supports transgender women of color who are still alive. The **Minister Bobbie Jean Baker Memorial Fund** is one such cause, though you should also take the time to research organizations doing vital work in your local area.

Plan an educational event that will help your congregation become more aware and connected in your local community. Invite local transgender leaders to come and talk about their lives and the challenges they face. Compensate them for their time and emotional labor. Support their work throughout the year.

Appendix B:

Supporting Black Transgender Women
By Chris Paige

> *Love is a call as well as a response,*
> *but, most of all, love is an action.*
>
> **Angelica Ross**

I have talked in this volume about the impact of violence on transgender women of color. Yet, many of us who want to be allies to transgender women of color struggle to make our work relevant. This appendix compiles some advice and insight offered by several Black transgender women in the hopes that all of us can become more effective allies.

I am following the basic outline of an article by Angelica Ross in the 2013 *Transgender Day of Remembrance Toolkit* created by Transfaith and the Trans People of Color Coalition—because her practical advice is useful even beyond Transgender Day of Remembrance efforts. Ross offered five points of advice toward supporting transgender women of color: Reach Out, Be More Than an Ally, Extend Your Privilege, Raise Awareness, and Love Is an Action.

The first point from Ross ("Reach Out") broke down some very practical considerations:

> In many cities, social services, programs, and LGBT religious organizations are located in areas where there are not many people of color. ... Rainbow stickers and symbols are not enough to reach out to transgender women and communicate to them that they are welcome. (Angelica Ross)

How are people of color treated in the neighborhood(s) around our events and activities? Is there public transportation for those who cannot afford a vehicle or ride share? How will transgender women of color learn about our efforts? Are we plugged into the networks that they frequent?

In a 2020 video by *The Root*, Diamond Stylz offered important insight into dynamics around Black trans women in terms of how race, gender, intimate partner violence, family rejection, community trauma, poverty, and underemployment conspire to turn Black transgender women into casualties:

> All oppression is connected. ... Because of our lack of economic [and] social mobility, we don't have certain protections to keep us safe ... [T]here are so many levels to why men uphold patriarchy. ... [T]hey are scared, they are fearful, they are so policed in so many different ways. [So that] when they lash out, when they haven't worked through their trauma, when they haven't worked through their exploration, when they don't have anybody to talk to about this without being judged, usually we are the ones who have to be the ones ... [We end up being] the person there who gets the negative, when there is someone who is traumatized and trying to deal with this stuff. (Diamond Stylz)

With such a complex array of contributing factors, there is no quick fix. However, there are many opportunities for allies to provide support. In Ross's article, her second point ("Be More Than an Ally") made the connections between being an ally and being a friend:

> In other words, build real relationships. The world is a better place when you've got friends. As a friend, you enter into someone's life and can make a difference on the good days and the bad ones. Many transgender women of color have lost loved ones to anti-transgender violence. Others of us fear that violence in our lives on a daily basis and are vulnerable because we are so isolated from social support. (Angelica Ross)

In a follow-up to a 2017 "Do ALL Black Lives Matter?" live broadcast, Dee Dee Watters discussed the social dynamic in her own way:

> When Black trans women are murdered, the reason it's so shocking [is because] ... a Black trans women's experience is completely different. We [often] don't have the ability to speak out and tell our stories—and even worse, when we do tell our stories, our LGBT counterparts and trans brothers wind up frowning upon us for telling our authentic and true stories. ... One of the main [supportive] things would be to create space

> and affirm that space for us to be there and feel like we can be our authentic selves and tell our truths and our stories. (Dee Dee Watters)

This dynamic raises important questions for allies: How do our efforts support the development of new relationships? How are we moving toward being a meaningful part of the lives of transgender women of color? How are we making space for uncomfortable truths to be told? Are we actually ready to show up when a friend or colleague is in crisis?

In Ross's third point ("Extend Your Privilege"), she suggested that we each check "the temperature of any space we are in, especially public spaces." Each of us needs to learn to use our resources (for example, power, access, wealth, relationships, and social familiarity) to

> decrease the pain that another person might experience in that space and increase their agency. Think of (or learn about) the many social activities or basic tasks that may be challenging for transgender women of color—and find a way to extend your privilege to make things a little less challenging. (Angelica Ross)

I want to acknowledge that extending privilege in this way requires some skillfulness. Appropriate intervention skills may not be obvious to those of us who live our lives farther from harm's way. Becoming relevant may mean learning new tactics for offering support without taking over a situation—without escalating or becoming a "savior" figure in ways that further disempower those who are already targets. Again, this is not a quick fix, but it is something for which each one of us should be working to be better prepared.

Education and awareness are often lifted up as ways that allies can support transgender people generally. In her "Raise Awareness" section, Ross said, "[K]now the facts, and share that knowledge." For example, we can become familiar with laws and policies in our area (that either target or support transgender folk). Research existing support and advocacy resources, too. Not all health clinics and shelters are prepared to support transgender women of color. Mental health, legal, clothing, and even food resources may be ill-prepared, if not antagonistic, to transgender women of color. Find out who is ready to provide trans-competent and racially sensitive care. Listen and learn about what our communities are really like for transgender people (and transgender women of color in particular). Look into what local resources (both individual people and formal programs) are already known for supporting transgender women of color. Finding ways to support those resources personally is a great way to start.

It is critically important for allies to find out where transgender leaders are already working locally. When we are not part of the communities that are most impacted, then it is essential and necessary for us to support the leadership of those who are. It is rarely helpful for allies to launch new, independent campaigns when we could be joining with *existing* efforts to address incidents, patterns of harassment, discrimination, and violence. Meanwhile, stay aware that the politics of supporting transgender women of color may be more complicated than simply being an ally to transgender people more generally. For instance, work on issues of street harassment, sexual assault, and police profiling will disproportionately impact transgender women of color, even though other segments of transgender communities may make these issues a low priority.

The fifth point in Ross's article ("Love Is an Action") was a helpful reminder that good intentions and goodwill are not sufficient. How are we *acting* to honor the leadership of transgender women of color in our areas? How are we *providing tangible support* for those who are most vulnerable? How are we *inviting* transgender women of color to share their stories of loss or survival—and are we *compensating* them for their time and emotional labor? How are we *working in solidarity* with transgender women of color who are moving into new kinds of strength and empowerment?

Both Watters and Ross are entrepreneurs who have worked on employment issues, each in her own way. In another interview, Watters said, "We talk about how Black trans women are getting paid less than $10,000 per year, but no one says 'Let me help you get a job.'" She suggests that providing employment opportunities for Black trans people is a critical issue in shifting the dynamics at play in the lives of transgender women of color. Employment leads toward financial independence, which can in turn remove (or at least reduce) many other risk factors. Allies need to move beyond sending good energy from afar toward actually providing opportunities where transgender women of color can thrive as productive members of the community.

Making a commitment to transgender women of color cannot be business as usual. In this reflection, I have highlighted wisdom from several Black transgender women who are from the United States. Other transgender women of color (Black and not Black, American and not American) may have other insights and needs. There are a variety of ways that institutions punish transgender women of color for surviving, including abuse for those who are incarcerated. Language, culture, documentation, and asylum may be important areas of concern for some. War and environmental devastation are impacting many communities around the world, creating new challenges for transgender women of color in those places.

Of course, there is no way that any ally can be an expert in all of these areas of concern. That is not my point. Rather, if we are not already woven into the lives of transgender women of color, we probably need to get more familiar with different neighborhoods and networks and institutions and issues. We will need to do research and learn new skills to make ourselves relevant. Understanding the ways that many factors conspire to put transgender women of color at risk is essential to that process, but we cannot break through their isolation while seated on the sidelines far removed from their circumstances.

Please look for the following sources of this article. Each one is worth your review!

"How Can I Help? Taking Transgender Women of Color Seriously" (Transfaith TDOR toolkit) by Angelica Ross.

"*Marsha's Plate* Trans Podcast Wants to Liberate All Black People" (*The Root, January 21, 2020*) by Terrell Jermaine Starr (featuring Diamond Stylz with a video profile).

Interviews with Dee Dee Watters at Transfaith: "A Prayer for Black Trans Women" and "Focus on the Individual: Five Questions with Dee Dee Watters."

The recording of the "Do ALL Black Lives Matter?" live broadcast (with Dee Dee Watters, Monica Roberts, and Diamond Stylz) is a related resource, available on the YouTube channel for Diamond Stylz.

I also recommend that you follow and support Black Trans Women, Inc. (http://www.blacktranswomen.org) and Trans Tech Social Enterprises (http://www.transtechsocial.org).

The *Marsha's Plate* podcast includes a regular transgender 101 segment as well as coverage of culture that will provide further insight.

Appendix C

Liturgical Resources

We Gather

By Louis Mitchell

We gather to remember
Your vibrant light and your soaring laughter
We gather to remember
The hands you held and lives you touched
We gather to remember
Your uncommon tenderness and your unwavering strength
We gather to remember
The sunrises that we greeted in revelry and the sunsets that we christened with our tears.

We gather to remember
That your essence will never be just a statistic, a number, a headline
Your life was too big for that
You are not just an unsolved case or a misgendered news article
You are my sister, my brother, my kindred.

I'll hear you in the rustle of a skirt
I'll smell you in the warmth of my grandmother's kitchen
I'll taste you in the saltiness of my tears
I'll see you in the flowers' new bloom
I'll feel you in the heat of an embrace.

We are the stones that the builders rejected
We are the honey in the lion's belly
We are the sword in the stone
We are the rose that blooms in winter
We are the fresh spring in the desert.

Common and unique

Mundane and magical
Secular and sacred
Visible and hidden
Frightened and courageous
Endangered and eternal,

No song can fully contain the music of us
No portrait can fully capture the beauty of us
No law can regulate us out of existence
No act of harm can extinguish the flame of us,

Together, we grow supple and strong
Nurtured by our many gifts
Watered by our tears of becoming
Though pruned by circumstances
We continue to bloom anew
In every season.

We are truth embodied
We are the intersections of all that is and ever was
The tapestry we weave with our lives,
Multi-textured and vibrant,
Is the answer to questions, ancient and yet to come.

In our authenticity, in our joy,
Even in the midst of hardship
We are the embodiment of creation
Birthing a world and a time
Of safety, self-determination
Of love and celebration.

We gather to bear witness to our grief and anger together
Today we read these names with heavy hearts
We gather to celebrate you and your life
Knowing that your seeds have been planted
We gather to see the faces of those that remain
Trusting our ability to nurture each other
We gather to show the world
A time when there will be no need for this way of naming us

We gather to show the world and each other
That all of our lives are valuable.

Copyright 2013 by Louis Mitchell. All rights reserved. Reprinted with permission from the author. Originally written for TDOR Unite! Transgender Day of Remembrance 2013 online service. Available at https://www.youtube.com/watch?v=-LXkMgl-WWI. The entire "Our Lives are Valuable" service is also available as a playlist on YouTube.

The Beatitudes, Re-imagined
By J Vu Mai and Alexx Anderson

Blessed are you who find beauty outside of the gender binary.
Blessed are you who are constantly misgendered.

Blessed are you who assert your pronouns even when you're tired.
Blessed are you who cherish your energy when the world tries your spirit.

Blessed are you who stay resilient in your fluidity.
Blessed are you who live unapologetically in glitter and rainbows.

Blessed are you who embrace the nuances of identity.
Blessed are you who struggle to survive in a body that makes you uncomfortable.

Blessed are you who thrive in the midst of uncertainty.
Blessed are you who embrace the body that liberates your colorful spirit.

Blessed are you who are transitioning in the midst of condemnation and turmoil.
Blessed are you who occupy transphobic pulpits and speak truth to power.

Blessed are you who endure traumatic binaries that discount your experience.
Blessed are you who are erased in conversations of gender justice.

Blessed are you who are forced to choose a label that constricts the air you breathe.
Blessed are you who stretch spiritual imaginations.

Blessed are you who twist and bend and transform normative ways of worship.
Blessed are you who recognize gender-bending as Divine expansiveness.

For since the image of G-d is in all of us, we are birthed into G-d's grace.

Copyright 2019 by J Vu Mai and Alexx Anderson. All rights reserved. Reprinted with permission of the authors. Originally developed for a practical theology seminary class focused on trauma in which there had been no discussion of queer and trans lives.

Embodied Remembrance: The Sacredness of Trans Day of Remembrance
By RJ Robles

Leader: Spirit, for the gift of life that is precious and life-giving, we are thankful. To have life and breath, to love and have being, to resist.

All: We give thanks for our strength, for the precious ability to love, and for those who answer your calling to live fully as Your trans sisters, brothers, and siblings.

Leader: For when there is darkness in our lives, drenched in white supremacy and transphobia—from the micro and macro aggressions we experience on a day-to-day basis, we ask for your protection. Spirit, guide and hold us in the midst of chaos.

All: We give you thanks for our chosen families, lovers, friends, communities, and accomplices who have been with us, supporting us, lifting us up, and loving on us.

Leader: For those who have been murdered, lynched, and stabbed to death, we remember. We cry out for trans and racial justice! And we live our lives building solidarity, raising awareness, and seeking to do better. In their honor.

All: We give thanks for the people that have devoted their life's work to the prevention of trans violence, for those who support each gender transition, and for those who continue to show up in the lives of our transgender siblings.

Leader: Inspire us to challenge, ask the hard questions, educate and agitate, and to ultimately take a stand against the evils that allow the violence to continue—stigma, fear, discrimination, resentment, and death-dealing systems and structures of oppression.

All: In the sacred presence of our newly arrived ancestors and those who have come before us, we cherish the memories of those we have lost and dream of a world where we can all be free.

Leader: To you, we lift up our dreams for a different world, where violence no longer exists, where there is access to life-giving care, and where transphobia comes to a radical stopping end.

All: Our dreams of liberation,

Leader: Our dreams of a world where all of your trans kindred are honored.

All: A collective vision of freedom we know you share.

Copyright 2019 by RJ Robles. All rights reserved. Reprinted with permission of the author. Originally written for worship at New Covenant Christian Church (Disciples of Christ), Nashville TN.

A Prayer with Black Trans Women
By Dee Dee Watters

   Father God, Mother God, Amazing God, God of Gods—my Alpha, my Omega, my Beginning, my End, my First, my Last—the very reason why I have breath,
   I come to you asking that you receive my sisters—that you allow my sisters to be welcomed into your arms, your welcome and your arms that are Love. The arms that should be the same arms of love—that should be down here on this earth, that are open and welcoming.
   We scream about the Bible and we scream about the church, but we don't scream about the Love that is supposed to be held within. One of the easiest things, one of the cheapest things, one of the freest things to do is to love. So, I speak of love and I speak of loving.
   I hope that those who [read] this today will experience this love and compassion that was given through our words. I hope that they will be able to receive that love from us as Black trans women. We *love* you. And there's not much that you can do about it to change it.
   I am speaking this prayer to speak it into existence that better days are coming, that the love of God will be our light at the darkest hour. We have gathered to mourn the loss of trans children. Someone's child that has been murdered. Someone's sister has been murdered. Someone's niece has been murdered. Someone who could have been the next *somebody* has been murdered. And, if you know like I know, you could have been murdered, too!
   We mourn. We hug. We love. We rest. Now, it's time for us to stop doing the same old things. It is o.k. to rest, but we need to wake up on the next day and get started on our journey, because this is a battle. This is a war that we must fight. The only way that we can fight is if we have enough soldiers to fight this battle with us.
   So, continue to stand with us. Start to understand that we are being murdered. Again, I am speaking into existence in this prayer—that our allies step up and become comrades. That we will have those

who were scared to say something [and] didn't want to stand and fight for us to become allies. We need their voices and we need yours

Father God, we come to you. Mother God, we come to you. Sister God, we come to you. Brother God, we come to you. Best friend God, we come to you.

We ask that you allow our siblings to love on us the way that we love on them. To show up the way that we show up. To show out whenever we need them to show out. Most importantly, not everyone has the courage to fight, but we all have the ability to LOVE! So love us the way that we deserve to be loved—not half way, but all the way.

Father God, we thank you for being a God who loves us. Mother God, we thank you for sending your only begotten son Jesus just for us.

In reality, we live in God's beautiful image. Please remind folk that we were not created to be hated, but we *are* different. We just want to be ourselves and to be loved in our genuine and authentic truth. We deserve that.

In the name of Jesus, I pray this prayer. In the name of Jesus, I ask that you release these spirits and allow them to be at rest. In the name of Jesus, allow each and every person that is [reading] to know that there is no reason to feel alone and scared, but allow that fear to be ammunition to speak truth to power.

What do we do? What will we do? We will believe. We will grow. We will come together. We will plan. We will strategize. We will overcome this. We will do this, not only with the love of God, but with the love of our allies, our friends, and our supporters. We love you all.

Father God, Mother God, we thank you. Ancestors who came before us, we thank you. Leaders who have fallen and are fighting right now, we thank you. To those murdered and taken from us too soon we #SayTheirNames. We honor you!

To those who are scared right now, we encourage you and thank you for living your life and your truth. We hope that you know that you are not alone. We thank God because tomorrow is a new day with new and old opportunities and, hopefully, on that day you will start over, too. You will be able to live your life, not in fear, but with pride.

Amen. Ashe.

Copyright 2017 by Dee Dee Watters. All rights reserved. Printed with permission of the author. Adapted from live broadcast, "Do ALL Black Lives Matter?" (with Dee Dee Watters, Monica Roberts and Diamond Stylz) on the YouTube channel of Diamond Stylz.

Standing Against the Headwind of Hatred
A Prayer of Cisgender Confession and Commitment
by Tammerie Day

> *We are experiencing a headwind of hatred*
> *and intolerance in the United States.*
>
> **Assistant Attorney General Thomas Perez,**
> **Civil Rights Conference on Hate Crimes (2011),**
> **University of Texas at Arlington**

We rise each day into a world that fits
Our natures, our understandings, our assumptions.
The clay of our bodies and faces
Conform to our spirits:
      male, female.

We are learning that it is not so for all of us.
Some of us are born of a wilder imagination.
We are learning new language and new images
For those Spirit is coloring outside our lines:
      transgender, intersex, gender-variant.

We confess that we have slumbered
While members of our family are slaughtered.
The headwind of hatred batters
Bodies and minds and spirits:
      the diverse beauties that continue to arise.

We commit to standing against this headwind of hate,
      a bulwark to end the battering.
We commit to seeing the diverse beauty, all around us,
      every gendered and gender-free expression, every form of love.

We commit to loving difference, and becoming.
We commit to learning the new language(s)
      that enable our beloveds to exist, and thrive.

Love, make us bold, to live our own lives fully and abundantly.
Love, give us passion, to work for everyone's full abundance.
Love, gather us together, so that no one you have created
      is not seen
      is not allowed to live
      is ever lost to the hurricane of hate again.

Copyright 2012 by Tammerie Day. All rights reserved. Reprinted with permission from the author.

Acknowledgements

I want to acknowledge that, more than my own individual insight, this volume reflects my own synthesis of the collective wisdom held carefully within transgender communities. While these explorations reflect my own particular perspective and credit specific sources, I am also indebted and grateful to all those who have endured, lamented, and remembered before me. As always, I write for those who are yet to come.

Minister Bobbie Jean Baker is a treasure. I am proud and thankful to have known her. I am also grateful to the Awards Committee of the Minister Bobbie Jean Baker Memorial Fund who provide wisdom as to how Transfaith can best serve our communities, while keeping Bobbie Jean's memory alive. It is my privilege to serve in support of them and the awardees.

I am grateful for Kylar Broadus, Louis Mitchell, J Mase III, and Angelica Ross, who each played important roles in the development of the *Transgender Day of Remembrance Toolkit*, from which some of the content in this booklet has been drawn.

I am grateful to Crystal Cheatham (*Our Bible App*), Alison Amyx (*Believe Out Loud*), and Cathy Knight (Church within a Church movement) who each, in their editorial capacities, invited me to find words to share. In particular, I want to acknowledge the following previous publications:

> "Observance" is adapted from "Ten Things Every Ally Should Know about Transgender Day of Remembrance" by Mx Chris Paige, which was published first at Transfaith and soon after in a Christianized form at *Believe Out Loud* in 2013.

> "Bearing Witness" is adapted from "An Open Letter to Our Allies about What We Really Need from You," co-authored by Mx Chris Paige, Dr. Donovan Ackley III, and Mr. Z Shane Zaldivar and published at *Transfaith* in 2017.

> "Resistance" and "Repentance" are adapted and expanded from "Claiming Our Mourning, Claiming Our Resistance" by Mx Chris Paige, published in the newsletter of the Church within a Church movement in 2018, as well as at *Transfaith*.

> "Vigilance," "Lamentation," and "Resilience" previously appeared in

Our Bible App as a three-day devotional by Mx Chris Paige in 2019 and were revised slightly for use in this edition.

Specific contributions, directly and indirectly, by other authors are acknowledged by name near the relevant text in this volume. I am grateful that Louis, J, Alexx, RJ, Dee Dee, and Tammerie thought it not robbery to allow for their work to be shared in Appendix C. We are all better for having access to their work.

I am also grateful to those who helped me birth this particular volume. To Mykal Shannon, my steady midwife, for providing feedback and encouragement. To Diane Owens who provided feedback and encouragement on both text and cover alternatives. To Ron Paige and Carolyn Paige, not only for making me, but for sticking with me and offering endless support, including as early readers. To Diamond Stylz for reviewing and offering feedback on the final manuscript. To Nancy Krody for her expert copy editing advice, once again.

He is mentioned elsewhere, but I also want to acknowledge the wisdom of Dr. Daniel Foor and the way that his teachings about the ancestors have opened up important insights for me that my Christian up-bringing did not provide. Thank you. All are encouraged to visit https://ancestralmedicine.org/ to learn more about his work.

Last, but not least, I am grateful for Louis Mitchell—my brother and friend—who once again provided valuable support in bringing this project to fruition. More generally, I have listened to him as he has observed, endured, remembered, borne witness, lamented, and OtherWise stayed vigilant for our communities. I have watched personally for a decade now, though he was at it long before I met him. Louis, I continue to learn from your wisdom, and it is a privilege to be a part of your one-day-at-a-time choices to live. Most of all, thank you for teaching me through your example. It is hard to imagine this booklet existing without your influence in my life.

With a full heart,

Mx Chris Paige

OtherWise Reflection Guides
from OtherWise Engaged Publishing

Christian Faith and Gender Identity: An OtherWise Reflection Guide (2019) by Mx Chris Paige is an entry-level resource, which provides a gentle introduction to transgender experience in the context of Christian tradition. This booklet includes scripture, modern definitions, reflection questions, and more.

In Remembrance of Me, Bearing Witness to Transgender Tragedy: An OtherWise Reflection Guide (2020) is a series of short meditations that unpack deep wisdom around themes such as grief, self-care, repentance, and our ancestral traditions. The booklet includes reflection questions and additional resources, including liturgical resources.

Paperback books are available from the publisher at a discount if you order multiple copies.

Sign up for updates from OtherWise Engaged Publishing to hear about other new releases as they become available!

Please visit http://otherwiseengaged4u.wordpress.com to learn more.

The OtherWise Christian series
from OtherWise Engaged Publishing

OtherWise Christian: A Guidebook for Transgender Liberation (2019) by Mx Chris Paige is a more in-depth resource that looks at 25 years of transgender-affirming biblical scholarship and includes an extensive bibliography of additional resources. There is also a free *OtherWise Christian* group discussion guide. Mx. Chris Paige argues that the Bible shows us story after story of OtherWise-gendered people being used by God to further the kingdom. Yet, we have been bamboozled by a restrictive gender ideology that is aligned with empire, white supremacy and Christian supremacy. Jesus and our biblical ancestors invite us to join a gender-full resistance!

Watch for the forthcoming *OtherWise Christian 2: Stories of Resistance*. Mx Chris Paige has gathered together 30 transgender, non-binary, two spirit, and intersex authors to share about their lived experience in relationship with Christian tradition. Having provided a detailed survey of relevant scripture in *OtherWise Christian*, Mx Chris now brings us a survey of testimonies from actual OtherWise Christians in this new book due out in spring 2020 (wherever you buy books or ebooks). Reminding us that the discussion of gender issues is not a theoretical one, this collection provides insights into the ways that Christian tradition has served as both an obstacle and a resource for OtherWise-gendered people in the modern world.

Paperback books are available from the publisher at a discount if you order multiple copies.

Sign up for updates from OtherWise Engaged Publishing to hear about other new releases as they become available!

Please visit http://otherwiseengaged4u.wordpress.com to learn more.

About the Author: Mx Chris Paige

Mx Chris Paige is the author of *OtherWise Christian: A Guidebook for Transgender Liberation*, publisher of OtherWise Engaged Publishing, and blogs daily at otherwisechristian.com. Mx Chris was founding executive director of Transfaith and publisher of *The Other Side* magazine. They are available for speaking, teaching, and preaching engagements.

Praise for OtherWise Christian

"In this invigorating dive into scripture ... Paige reads the Bible in provocative ways to affirm support for transgender experience. ... surprising yet plausible. ... strong and imaginative. This is a treasure chest of resources for those interested in ways transgender individuals can live faithful to God and to one's self."

Publishers Weekly

"This is the book that we need."

The Rev. Terri Stewart
United Methodist Alliance for Transgender Inclusion (UMATI)

"The most exhaustive look at gender non-conforming/trans identities in the Bible that I have seen to date. Informative & accessible."

Peterson Toscano
Transfigurations: Transgressing Gender in the Bible

"I am excited to revisit familiar characters and narratives with a new OtherWise lens. This is an extraordinary gift to the trans community and to those, whether transgender or cisgender, who wish to go deeper in the texts to see those of us who have been hidden, erased, and/or disparaged."

The Rev. Louis Mitchell
Executive Director of Transfaith

"... a truly incredible book. Mx Chris' writing is clear, elegant, and prophetic, and the book's intertextual readings of scripture and popular culture are very insightful. This book beautifully answers the deepest possible question: how can we imagine and practice our spirituality in ways that are truly just and liberatory, especially as it concerns our gender."

Cleis Abeni/Upāsikā tree
Transgender elder

"... a wonderful resource... This is a faith text that CANNOT be ignored."

The Rev. Shanea D. Leonard
Associate for Gender & Racial Justice for the Presbyterian Church (U.S.A.)

"... a brilliant yet down-to-earth, supremely compassionate and practical guide for how religious people who don't fit binary categories can engage with and draw strength from the Bible... "

Dr. Joy Ladin
The Soul of the Stranger: Reading God and Torah from a Transgender Perspective

OtherWise Engaged Publishing

OtherWise Engaged Publishing is excited to be working with the best and brightest of OtherWise-gendered folk! We provide a multi-tradition, independent publishing operation for projects from OtherWise-gendered folk that are in alignment with our values.

Visit otherwiseengaged4u.wordpress.com
for information about our latest releases
and to support independent transgender-led publishing.

What are the words you do not yet have?
What do you need to say?
What are the tyrannies you swallow day by day
and attempt to make your own,
until you will sicken and die of them, still in silence.

~ Audre Lorde